Safety

Jean Harrison

Safety

Jean Harrison

A⁺

Smart Apple Media

First published in 2004 by Evans Brothers Limited in association with Save the Children UK.
2A Portman Mansions
Chiltern Street
London, W1U 6NR

Published in the United States by Smart Apple Media
2140 Howard Drive West, North Mankato, Minnesota 56003

Library of Congress Cataloging-in-Publication Data

Harrison, Jean.
Safety / by Jean Harrison.
p. cm. — (Children's rights)
Includes index.
ISBN 1-58340-422-8
1. Accidents—Prevention—Juvenile literature. 2. Children's rights—Juvenile literature. I. Title. II. Series.

HV675.5.H37 2004
363.1'083—dc22   2004041700

9 8 7 6 5 4 3 2 1

Credits:

Series editor: Louise John
Editor: Nicola Edwards
Designer: Simon Borrough
Producton: Jenny Mulvanny

Acknowledgements
Cover: Kalpesh Lathigra
Title page: Kalpesh Lathigra
p6: Brendan Paddy/SCUK
p7: Stuart Freedman/Network
p8: Dan White/SCUK
p9: Anne Heslop
p10: Michael Amendolia/Network
p11a: Michael Amendolia/Network
p11b: Michael Amendolia/Network
p12: Michael Amendolia/Network
p13: Michael Amendolia/Network
p14: Tim Hetherington/Network
p15a: Tim Hetherington/Network
p15b: Tim Hetherington/Network
p16: Sebastian Rich/SCUK
p17: Jenny Matthews
p18: Tim Hetherington/Network
p19: Tim Hetherington/Network
p20: Stephen Lewis
p21: Dario Mitidieri
p22: Kalpesh Lathigra
p23: Kalpesh Lathigra
p24: Howard Davies
p25a: Michael Amendolia/Network
p25b: Dan White
p26: Stuart Freedman/Network
p27a: Stuart Freedman/Network
p27b: Stuart Freedman/Network

Contents

All children have rights   6

Children who are poor have the right
to be safe   8

Cristian's story   10

Children who work have the right
to be safe   12

Amadou's story   14

Children caught up in war have
the right to be safe   16

Jueir's story   18

All children, including girls, have
the right to be safe   20

Bhumisar's story   22

Children who are surrounded by
violence have the right to be safe   24

Rosa's story   26

Glossary   28

Index   29

Additional information   30

All children have rights

The history of rights for children In 1919, a remarkable woman named Eglantyne Jebb wanted to help children who were dying of hunger as a result of World War I. She founded an organization in the United Kingdom called the Save the Children Fund. Four years later, she wrote a special set of statements: a list of children's rights. Jebb said that her goal was "to claim certain rights for children and labor for their universal recognition." This meant that she wanted worldwide agreement on children's rights.

It was many years before countries around the world agreed that children have rights, but eventually the statements became recognized in international law in 1989. They are now known as the United Nations Convention on the Rights of the Child (UNCRC). The rights in the UNCRC are based on the idea that everyone deserves fair treatment.

Almost every country has signed the UNCRC, so it affects most of the world's children. The rights it lists cover all areas of children's lives, such as the right to have a home and the right to be educated.

In times of war, families, such as this one in Afghanistan, can find it hard to protect their children from the dangers that are around them.

Children in many parts of the world, like these in Honduras, meet to learn about their rights.

Rights for all? The UNCRC should mean that the rights of children everywhere are guaranteed. However, this is not the case. Every day, millions of children are denied their rights. Children may suffer discrimination because they are poor or disabled, or because they work for a living. It might be because of their religion, race, or whether they are boys or girls.

Children are very vulnerable, so they need special care and protection. The UNCRC exists to try to make sure that they are protected.

The right to feel safe Many of the articles in the UNCRC are about every child's right to feel safe and protected. When children feel safe, they are able to grow into healthy and useful citizens. Here are some of the articles:

Article 19 You have the right to protection from injury, violence, abuse, and neglect.

Article 22 You have the right to special protection and help if you are a refugee.

Article 32 You have the right to protection from work that is bad for your health or education.

Article 38 You have the right to not be in an army or fighting in a war before you are 15. If you are affected by war, you must be protected.

This book tells the stories of children around the world who are achieving their rights.

Children who are poor have the right to be safe

"There's a lot of fighting around here—so much you sometimes can't even go out of your house." Juan, 9, Colombia

Feeling safe It is important for everybody to live in safety, not just those who have money. It is particularly important for children to live in places where they are protected from danger. Children need people who will look after them if they hurt themselves or if they are afraid or in danger. It is the children from poor families who are most often denied their right to live in a place of safety.

Unsafe places Children who are poor are more likely to live in unsafe places. The building they live in may be poorly constructed, or old and falling down. It may be in an area where there are dangerous chemicals, or on land that is likely to flood and so is unsuitable for houses. In places like this, the rent is lower, so people who have little money are more likely to go there to live. Children who live in dangerous places are more likely to get sick or have accidents.

The parents of this family in East Timor, where a peace-keeping force is needed, struggle to give their children a safe place to live.

Leaving home Some children leave home because they are badly treated or because their parents can't afford to look after them. In many big cities across the world, children live on the streets, where their health and safety are at risk.

8

Many children's lives are affected when there is an emergency in their country. In times of war, or when a disaster such as an earthquake or flood occurs, it can become too dangerous to stay at home, so they have to find a safer place to live until the emergency is over.

Dangerous jobs Many poor children have to work—sometimes in dangerous conditions. Their employer may not provide machinery and tools that are safe to use or give them special clothing and equipment, such as goggles, that protect them from harmful chemicals, sounds, or lights. Children in particular are likely to get sick when they live or work in poor conditions, because their bodies are still growing and are weaker than adults' bodies.

Feeling scared Children can easily become frightened, especially if other people treat them badly. All children have the right to be looked after and protected by adults.

Bad weather and disasters can rob children of a safe place to live. This family has found a temporary home after an earthquake destroyed their home in Gujerat, India.

Cristian's story

Eleven-year-old Cristian lives in Medellin, a city in the South American country of Colombia. It is one of the most violent places in the world. Cristian's home is in a part of town where gangs fight each other, mainly over drugs and money.

One day Cristian was out with his mom when they saw some young men with guns run down the road. Cristian knew they were gang members, and he hurried his mom inside the house. A few minutes later, they heard shooting, and not long after that, the police came. The gang members had shot and killed a man. Cristian was very frightened but relieved that he and his mom had managed to get out of the way.

Many people in the neighborhood were getting worried about the gangs. They saw that children were imitating the gang members, fighting and bullying each other.

Cristian shoots baskets with his friends Wilmer and Juan in the safety of the school playground.

So the local teachers started a project called *Living Together*. Through this project, the children began to learn to respect each other, even when they disagreed about things. They learned to talk to each other and to work together to solve their problems.

Cristian was chosen to be a class representative and attend some workshops. When he came back to his class, he told the other children what he had learned. Then they all tried to put the ideas into action.

The children have learned to play together without fighting each other.

One day Cristian was brave. He saw two boys pretending to strangle each other. Some other boys were trying to get them to fight each other for real. Cristian did an odd thing; he threw a bucket of cold water on them. The shock of the water was so great that the boys stopped fighting for a minute. Then Cristian said, "Don't fight any more—if you stop now, you'll soon forget about it and become friends again."

And that is exactly what happened. Cristian and his friends are much happier now that they are learning to make life safer for themselves and their families.

Cristian says, "I think my community can get rid of the gangs if people change and children are told to talk instead of fighting."

Children who work have the right to be safe

The need to work Most children work because they need to—their families need the money they earn to survive. Not all child labor is harmful. Some children stay at home and help with the family business, which might be a farm or a shop. Only about 1 out of 20 working children produces goods for export. Most work in family homes or businesses or as street vendors.

Health and safety In developed countries such as the United States, there are very strict "health and safety" laws to protect people in their places of work, in shops, and in other public places. Some countries do not have such laws or are too poor to enforce them. Some employers are more interested in making money than in making sure the workers are protected. Many people, including children, in less developed countries such as India or Mali have to work in unsafe conditions.

Twelve-year-old Anh sells lottery tickets in the market district of Ho Chi Minh City in Vietnam.

"I don't like the work at all, but we wouldn't be able to eat if I didn't work." Guddi, 16, India

Unsafe working conditions

Some children are exploited. They may have to work full-time when they are very young, or may not be paid fairly for their work or treated well.

They may have to work long hours with no breaks and in places where there is little fresh air. The long hours mean that the children cannot go to school or are too tired to learn. They may have little time to relax and play. Some of the materials the children work with may be dangerous and make them sick. Children like Guddi from India work in small, dark, airless rooms heating glass bracelets over a hot flame.

Away from home

Some children, such as those who make carpets in India and Pakistan, have to leave home to work. Some of them have even been kidnapped or sold and taken far away from home to provide cheap labor for their employers.

Finding a better life

Projects have been set up to improve the lives of working children. They help families find ways of earning more money and help the children go to school so that they can get good jobs when they are grown up.

Fabiana and her friend Ilka in Brazil both work as baby-sitters even though they are still children themselves.

Amadou's story

Amadou approached the hillside cautiously. He was the first to arrive at the gold mine in Burkina Faso, West Africa, where he spent several hours every day underground. Would there be any problems today? The entrance to the mine was just a narrow hole in the ground. So many children went through it each day that the edges had had to be strengthened with sandbags. But if the sandbags became loose and fell into the mine, there would be no way out for anyone inside.

Amadou adjusted the flashlight tied to his head and carefully lowered himself through the rough opening. He paused for a moment to let his eyes adjust to the darkness inside. He carefully felt his way down the shaft. He was looking for rocks that might have grains of gold in them. He had to hack the rocks from the sides of the shaft, carry them up to the surface, and then take them home to be crushed. Constant digging into the sides of the shaft to get the rocks out had made huge holes and tunnels. Twice, the roof had caved in and rocks and soil had tumbled down. When that happened, Amadou could only wait for the

The entrance to the mine is narrow and dangerous.

14

dust to settle and then dig up toward the surface, hoping that the way out had not been blocked.

Amadou had not been working in the mines for long. He used to watch his parents digging there and would then go down secretly after the adults had all left. Now he was 10 years old, and his parents had agreed that he was old enough to do this dangerous work. Adults now looked after the cattle, and boys went down the mine. Amadou's older sisters helped crush the rocks, then washed the pieces to find the gold.

Amadou began working. If he could get a good number of rocks out before the other boys came, there wouldn't be as much competition and he might be lucky enough to find some gold. Then he could take it and sell it in the market. The family badly needed the money it would bring.

Amadou says, "The reason we do this work is that we're trying to survive."

At the surface of the mine, the rocks are crushed and washed to find the gold.

Children's charities are working to help children like Amadou train for safer kinds of work, such as carpentry and motorcycle repair.

Children caught up in war have the right to be safe

War There are more than 50 major conflicts happening in the world today. Many of these conflicts are civil wars—wars that happen within a country rather than against another country. Most civil wars occur in the poorest countries of the world. They are the result of struggles between people who want to rule the country. Many children die or are injured in these wars. Nine out of 10 people killed in today's wars are civilians who are not directly involved in the fighting.

Forced to fight In recent years, thousands of children under 16 have been child soldiers. This is often because they have lost their families and have nowhere else to go. Their parents may have been killed in the fighting or have somehow become separated from them. Becoming a soldier may be the only way to get food and clothing. Sometimes children start out as messengers but end up as soldiers. Children who have been soldiers have seen so much suffering and death that they find it hard to return to normal life.

Aid workers help former child soldiers adjust to ordinary life and deal with all that they have experienced.

Young boys are often recruited into the armies of poor countries. These recruits are in Afghanistan.

"If it wasn't for the money, I would never have joined the army." Jueir, 11, Democratic Republic of Congo

Land mines There may be as many as 110 million land mines in more than 70 countries waiting to be stepped on. Although mines weigh as little as a bag of candy, each one holds enough explosive to blow off a leg if someone steps on it. Around 2,000 people—many of them children—are involved in land mine accidents every month. Around 800 of them will die, and the rest are badly hurt. Animals cannot graze, and farmers cannot plow land until all the mines have been cleared away.

Did you know?
In the last 10 years, two million children have died in wars, and another 4.5 million have been injured.

Refugees When there is war, many people have to leave their homes to find a safer place to live. It is mostly women and children who become refugees or are displaced because of war. Thousands of refugees are children who have become separated from their families. Being a refugee keeps children from doing normal things such as going to school and playing with friends.

Refugees waiting to return to their home country of Rwanda. Workers from relief agencies were on hand to help and protect any children who were traveling alone.

17

Jueir's story

Jueir lives in Kinshasa, the capital of the Democratic Republic of Congo. Although he is still only 11 years old, he has already been a soldier.

Jueir's father worked for the post office and was sent to a town called Kisangani. Jueir stayed behind with his aunt, who continued to look after him when his parents disappeared after war broke out.

Jueir's aunt is very poor, and it was hard for her to look after Jueir properly. He didn't go to school, and he had no job. One day, he heard that the army paid a monthly salary to all soldiers. Jueir decided to join the army, thinking it would be a good way to earn money. He was given a uniform and taught to march. The new recruits were given

Jueir, a former child soldier, is much happier growing vegetables.

jobs to do, such as preparing the meals and cutting firewood in the forest. But because they were not given any tools, it was hard work. They had to collect water in big containers and carry it long distances to where the soldiers were camping. If they didn't do this work, the boys were beaten.

Then the fighting came to the area where they were camping. Soldiers with serious wounds began to be brought in. Some had lost an arm or a leg, and there were even some dead bodies. The officers said that the boys would be the next to go to fight. Jueir was afraid. There was so much blood, and he didn't want to be killed. So, the next time he had to cut wood in the forest, he ran away, back to his aunt.

Now Jueir has joined a local group that is helping former child soldiers settle back into ordinary life. The boys are given small plots of land on which they can plant vegetables. When the vegetables are ready, the boys can take them home to help feed their families or can sell the produce to make money.

These former child soldiers are learning to grow vegetables.

In this way, the boys are able to support themselves and their families. The group also helps the children come to terms with their bad experiences in the army so that they can become part of their family and community again.

Jueir says, "In the army, they promised us $100 a month, but while I was there, I never saw that $100. At least here I see some money and I'm eating."

All children, including girls, have the right to feel safe

Growing up safely Although growing up can be difficult, most children and young people receive the love and care they need to become healthy adults. But some children are hurt, neglected, or abused by adults or other children. Some younger children may not realize that they are being abused because they have known no other life. Girls often receive more abuse than boys, partly because girls have often been seen as less important than boys. In the past, they were often allowed to work only at home or in other people's houses and did not earn much money. This is slowly changing as girls and women challenge the situation.

Bullying Some adults as well as children bully or frighten those who are smaller and weaker than themselves. Often this is because they feel unimportant and see this as a way to show that they are bigger and better than someone else. Girls are usually not as physically strong as boys and therefore can be more at risk of being bullied.

Children in this Colombian elementary school wear masks they have made. They learn how to overcome violence by acting out plays about their experiences of it.

"If girls become educated and there is equality, then violence will be less."
Bhumisar, 16, Nepal

20

Discrimination against girls For hundreds of years, girls and women have had to suffer discrimination by men and boys. They may have been harassed and mistreated. They may have been forbidden to go to school or to work. There are now laws against sexual harassment and inequality in many countries. But still, in many places in the world, men often treat women and girls badly. They do not give them the chance to work and be paid as equals.

Girls in poor countries often suffer from the prejudice of men. As members of a children's council, these girls in India are challenging this tradition.

21

Bhumisar's story

Bhumisar put the broom in the corner. It was still early morning at her home in Nepal, but she had already cleaned the whole house. Her next job was to collect water. The well was half an hour's walk from the village. Bhumisar dreaded the journey. She had to go alone and was scared the whole time she was away from the house. The path went past a small shop where men gathered to chat and drink tea. When Bhumisar walked past with her water pot, the men would often shout rude things or laugh at her. Sometimes men would follow her and she would have to run to leave them behind.

Bhumisar (on the left) with her friends. She says: "If girls unite in the village, things will continue to change."

There were other places in the village where girls felt scared —the forest, the crossroads, and neighbors' houses. Even going to one of the festivals could be dangerous. And it wasn't just the rude things the men said that scared girls. Sometimes, men would attack a girl who was out on her own.

The girls talked to each other about their problems and discovered that many of them felt scared. So they decided to make life safer for themselves. They made a list of the places and times when they felt scared. They talked about their experiences and realized that the men did not respect them or see them as equals. The traditional view was that girls and women were not important, and that they should stay at home to cook and clean.

The girls knew that this was wrong, but they also knew it would not be easy to change the way the men thought. So they began by talking with their parents. If their parents understood, then maybe they could talk to other adults and their sons to explain the need for change.

Then the girls began to get the boys at school involved. The boys saw that the girls' test scores were just as good as theirs. They saw the way the girls organized their meetings. They realized that girls were able to do more than cook and clean. They stopped taunting them and saying bad things about them.

The girls now have much more confidence in themselves. They even have the courage to go to the police if men have been violent.

Members of the girls' group playing with some of the younger children in the village.

Bhumisar has taken part in a project called *Safe Spaces for Girls*. She says, "I used to be shy and have low self-esteem. We organized a lot of meetings with parents and villagers, and my confidence grew."

Children who are surrounded by violence have the right to be safe

Surrounded by violence Children may be surrounded by violence even when there is no war in their country. They may live in an area where the streets are not safe. Maybe there are gangs who "rule" different streets and fight each other with guns and knives. Innocent people sometimes get hurt because they happen to be in the wrong place at the wrong time.

Missing school If children on their way to school have to walk past gangs fighting each other, the children may be shot by accident. Often, this danger means that children are kept at home, so they miss a lot of time at school. When this happens, it is hard to catch up on the work they have missed.

"In this country, the guerrillas, the army, the government, and the gangs have to learn to live together, but they want to fight each other until there's only one group left."
Wilmer, 11, Colombia

In some places, like this shantytown in Peru, it can be hard for children playing in the street to stay out of range of the guns of fighting gangs.

Imitating the gangs Children who live in areas where gangs threaten people's safety may grow up to imitate and then join gangs. They may not even realize that there is any other way to live.

It can be very hard for someone who lives in a violent area to avoid becoming involved in the violence. For example, fights are often about drugs. Poor people may be tempted to try taking drugs because they think it will help them cope with being poor. But drugs cost a lot of money. So they sell drugs to other people to try to earn some money. Selling drugs leads them into violence and makes their life worse.

This center used to be funded by Save the Children, but it is now self-supported.

Breaking the cycle of violence

Organizations such as Save the Children support groups that help children break away from the violence around them. They show them that a life without violence is better, help them get off the drugs they have been taking, and teach them the skills they will need to get a good job.

A worker from a project to help street children plays games with them. By making friends with the children, she is able to help them find a safe place to stay.

Rosa's story

Rosa now feels free to go out anywhere she wants. Her old gang realizes that she has found a better way to live.

Thirteen-year-old Rosa lives in San Pedro Sula, the second-largest city in Honduras, where she lives in one room with her parents and eight brothers and sisters.

Rosa sketched a final twirl on the design. It was perfect. Now she could transfer it onto the T-shirt she had made. She sat back and watched the others around the room. Some were drawing designs; others were sewing. They were her friends.

It was such a relief to have left her old life, as part of a gang, and feel safe instead of scared. "Why had I been crazy enough to join a gang?"

she asked herself. Well, it hadn't been easy to stay away. There were 10 gangs in the neighborhood. Her big brother Roberto belonged to one, and her sister Vanessa had joined another. The family was so poor that there was nothing at home for any of them, and at first it had been good to belong to a powerful group. You could get what you wanted, and no one dared stop you because you carried a gun or a knife.

But it was dangerous. The police and other gangs were often after you, and you never knew if you would be shot. It was like being in a trap. The gang leader wanted money every week.

There were so many guns, knives, and drugs, and Rosa had been scared nearly all the time.

Then she had met Susana, who worked with a project that was trying to persuade gang members that they could have a better life. Susana had told Rosa about the T-shirt-making shop, and Rosa had decided to try it. It had felt good to be learning useful skills. Rosa was glad that she had stuck to it, even though it had been hard. Now she had a goal in her life. She was going to finish school, buy a sewing machine, and set up her own business, making and selling clothes.

Rosa and her sister Vanessa have both managed to leave the gangs that were destroying their lives.

Rosa put her drawing pens away. The best thing about leaving the gang was getting to know her family again. Rosa knew that her mother still loved her, even though she had suffered so much.

Rosa says, "I feel useful now because I know how to do a few things and feel that people like me. I feel important."

27

Glossary

article A part of a legal document, such as a convention

child labor The work that children do when it is more than helping with ordinary household jobs

children's rights The rights that everyone under the age of 18 should have, including the right to life, the right to food, clothes, and a place to live, the right to education and health, and the right to be protected from danger

compensation Money given to make up for something bad that has happened to a person

conflict A serious disagreement between two or more groups of people that can lead to fighting

discrimination The unfair treatment of people because of their race, religion, or whether they are boys or girls

displaced people People who have had to leave their homes because of war or a natural disaster but stay within the same country

exploitation Unfairly taking advantage of a person; for example, if an employer pays children very little for working long hours in a factory

export To sell goods to another country

founded Started

harass To bother someone by repeatedly attacking (physically or verbally) him or her

hazardous Dangerous

illegal Against the law

less developed countries Countries that have few industries and in which many people are very poor

projects Plans set up to improve life for local people

recruit To persuade someone to join an organization

refugees People who leave their home country because they feel unsafe

representative Someone who is chosen by a group to speak on their behalf

shaft A tunnel in a mine

street vendors People who sell goods on the street rather than in shops

United Nations An organization made up of many different countries; it was set up in 1945 to promote international peace and cooperation

Index

abuse 20
accidents 8
Afghanistan 6, 16

Brazil 13
bullying 10, 20
Burkina Faso 14

chemicals 8
child soldiers 16, 18, 19
children's rights 6, 7, 8
civil wars 16
Colombia 8, 10, 20, 24
communities 11, 19
Congo, Democratic Republic
    of 16, 18

danger 8, 13, 14, 19, 22, 24
discrimination 6, 21
drugs 10, 25, 27

earthquakes 9
East Timor 8
emergencies 9

fighting 10, 11, 16, 19
floods 9

gangs 10, 11, 24, 25, 26, 27
girls' groups 23
gold mines 14, 15
Gujerat 9

harassment 21
Ho Chi Minh City 12
Honduras 26

India 9, 12, 13, 21

Jebb, Eglantyne 6

Kinshasa 18

land mines 17
laws 12, 21
Living Together project 11

Mali 12

Nepal 20, 22

Pakistan 13
Peru 24
poverty 6, 8, 9, 18, 21, 25, 27
projects 7, 11, 23

refugees 17
Rwanda 17

Safe Spaces for Girls project 23
Save the Children 6, 25
school 10, 13, 17, 18, 21, 23
street children 8, 25

UNCRC 6, 7
United Nations 6

Vietnam 12, 25
violence 10, 24, 25
    against girls 20, 21, 22, 23

West Africa 14
working children 9, 12
working conditions 9, 12, 13
World War I 6

Additional information

Books

Bennett, Paul. War: *The World Reacts*. North Mankato, Minn.: Smart Apple Media, 1999.

Castle, Caroline. *For Every Child: The UN Convention on the Rights of the Child*. New York: Dorling Kindersley Publishing, 2001.

Lobe, Tamara Awad. *A Right World: Helping Kids Understand the Convention on the Rights of the Child*. Washington, D.C.: Youth Advocate Program International, 1999.

Web sites

www.childrensrights.org/
The Children's Rights organization site

www.rcmp-grc.gc.ca/youth/childrights_c.htm
A site that explains the Rights of the Child in child-friendly language

www.savethechildren.org/
The Save the Children organization site

5.8/1